An Anthology of Anxious Anecdotes

Madison Wells

BookLeaf Publishing

Presentation by *BookLeaf Publishing*

Web: www.bookleafpub.com

E-mail: info@bookleafpub.com

ISBN: 9789357210508

First edition 2022

DEDICATION

For my mother, who has always encouraged and inspired my writing

to start.

Finding the place to start
in any adventure
is hard
daunting
overwhelming
flawed
confusing
and stress-inducing.
Starting is a pre-req
in success or failure.
In win
or loss,
in thriving
or
desperation,
exasperation.
How can I start
when I know there's an end?
In starting a poem
a story
a job
a meal
a craft
a trip
a love--
I'm starting somewhere
amidst this nowhere.

still starting.

Where's the start
And where's the end
And where's the in-between

Where're the breaks
And where's the line
Between prose and poetry

Who decides
Where stanzas stop
And where they pick back up

Who demands
A comma there,
A full stop. Or hiccup;

I'm in charge?
That can't be.
I just pick the spacing

I just start
A new line
To mix up the pacing.

What if I didn't and kept on going and stopped
making rhymes and rhythms and full stops and
hiccups and words and put down the pen

No poem
No sense made
No thoughts to attend

Then I guess
I've chosen
Where to start and end.

part one.

I don't understand football,
And I don't know how to play;
But when I think of life and death,
I like to think of them this way.

When Lil was born she joined the team
And had a very special task
She passed out cups and water
As she learned to catch and pass

Her teammates all took care of her,
both first and second string
And she spent most days practicing
with the others, too, in training

As she grew, she moved up the ranks
and one day she became tackle
She noticed the center, handsome and sweet
And knew together they'd work well

So with the blessing from her Coach, Center and Tackle
Became the Quarterbacks
I know that's not how the positions work,
But in this story it's of fact.

Not long after, they started a team of star players to be
They trained them every day and night
And watched them fight and lose and fight and win
Until they could hold the trophy upright.

They all passed through seasons undefeated
and had many championship stories to tell
Until one day when Mr. Quarterback was sacked
and on his back he fell

The whole team gathered on one knee
as the medics checked his vitals
But his concussion was bad and his future
on the team slowly became futile.

And so with that Coach pulled him out
And sat him on the side
So that he could watch his family
With a careful guiding eye.

ugly crier.

The dry paths of tears tighten my cheeks
They decorate my face with invisible stains
Pulling my skin into patterns of sadness
The salty, remnant puddles taunting my eyes

If the clouds are full
and the mood is right
Then droplets will fall
Heavy or light

The rain doesn't stop
So people can hide
It doesn't take breaks
So we stay warm and dry

Just as tears streak my swollen cheeks
And tattoo my face with patches of stains
Carving along features of sadness
The wasted water looming in my eyes

Once again

accepting imperfection.

Not everything must be impressive.
Simple effort will do just fine.
Relieving the mind from anxious burden,
Simple rhymes in simple lines.

once.

What was once concealed I am beginning to see.
What I once ignored is now directly in my path.
What once amounted from ignorance remains in
the past,
obliterated.
What I once proclaimed as truth is still truth,
but seen through different eyes.
What was once simple is now more complex;
what was complex is now simple.
I once was a girl, naive and bewildered.
I am now a woman, still naive and bewildered,
but with love.

part two.

Fifteen seasons came and passed
With Lil as the only quarterback
She ran and scored repeatedly
But she was starting to feel the slack

You see, Lil had a hard time seeing the ball
And it was hard to breathe while she ran
But she knew she couldn't step down from her throne
Until her daughter's young team was grown

Inevitably that time came and went
and she still played because she loved them
And as long as Lil was still around, no one could take her spot,
as she was as stubborn as she was a gem

So during a hot and humid game,
she saw an interception brewing on the field
And so she gave it everything she had
to keep the family's ball concealed

It took a lot
And she was breathing hard
But a cheer erupted in the stands.

She had run her longest yard

And regardless of the season score,
She knew that she had won.

spiritual contentment.

Adored, blessed, glorious, fantastical
Exposure to the great mystery of the ages
Your presence, Your love, truly ecclesiastical
Glory upon glory in the words on your pages.
Stratified, glorified, and never compromised
Help me in my journey to stay the course
Let me not find myself in front of the chariot of horses,
lest I be trampled.
Beatified, communion-ized, revolutionized
My portion is present in all that I sample.
You are my portion, so filling yet clandestine.
Endured, eternal, forgiving, and sacred
You are my everything
I shall let none take it.

spiritual discontentment.

I feel extremely disconnected,
away and misdirected,
pretending as if Your love is fake
and my reception's in distaste.
I'm tired and hungry
in body and soul
Both humanity and spirituality
take toll.
Help me to find You,
feel You,
in the darkness of selfishness,
materialism, idolatry, and carelessness.
Here I'm immersed in all that I want,
all that I need,
But I still consciously stand
against Your will and commands.
The façade is so beautiful
Sunshine wraps around me
but dark embers smoke within me.
Am I too hard on myself?
Not loving enough or too strict?
Help me to see You,
please crack through my shell
Before I time out of my clock's failing tick
and fall sin first into the hot flames of hell.

at the spiritual hospital.

There's a reason that you brought me here.
"The heart is what you do."
This matriarch speaks in seamlessly sewn words.
Forgive me, Lord, for I have sinned,
and fallen short of the Glory of God.
How many times have I calculated sin
and festered in the conniving ways of the
infected sores
created from the dull, ripping blades of Satan's
sword?
How many times have I come crawling like the
prodigal
with pockets empty and a charred heart,
and virtues slashed with stain?
I'm petty and I'm shallow.
I've let the world invade my my space
for far too long.
I come to you in need of healing,
at the bedside of your nurse.
Someday,
help me to help others
as many times as you've helped me.

snapshots.

Our minutes might be a candid image
and our hours a sketched portrait.
In a town of everlasting time,
not even the grandest film would suffice.
Maybe that is why souls do not linger-
they are far too glamorously intricate
to be caught on a fragile tape.
Their mere concept is enough to rip
our earthly reality to shreds.
Perhaps our dreams are the only images strong enough
to behold the glory of the afterlife's chosen.
But, who then scripts it?
What is divine, and what is of mind?
Only death, in all.

unrequited.

The agony of waiting for something to happen
that is never going to happen
is incomprehensible.
I think of all of the years that I waited
and waited and waited and waited
and waited
for something wonderful to happen--
and it simply didn't.
Not from lack of trying
but from a lack of fate.
Lack of a future together being written in the
stars
or in the cards
or in some divine plan.
Unrequitedness is a special pain
that cannot be matched.
The feeling of being unwanted by the person
you want most.

But it is how we grow,
and how we find our persons.

daughters and mothers.

Daughters,
Listen to your mothers
To their wisdom and advice
If they tell you to hold on
Then your strife is worth the fight
But if they say let go,
Release your bindings now.
They know your heart and mind
And that he isn't worth a cry.

Daughters,
Mothers love to hear your voice
Call when you're away and near-
They need to know you're safe
Their sleep matters not
When you're out with the moon
(Remember, mothers are daughters, too.)

Daughters,
Hug your mothers
Love your mothers
Sing with them in the car
Life is not forever
So make the most of it right now

Daughters,
Pray for your mothers
Because they've held you all through life
And someday,
When you're a mother too,
You'll want their prayers of wisdom and advice

part three.

When her final play was done
And the receiver was defeated,
Coach led her to the side,
Put his arm around her and said,

"You played a good game, Lil
You really gave it your all.
I know that some of those plays were tough
And that it wasn't always that easy to get up.

But, hey, you scored so many touchdowns
And led your team to greatness.
You gave the other team an iron fist
And you'll sure as hell be missed."

She didn't want to quit so soon or watch
in the stands as her husband had done.
But then she thought watching
with him would be so much fun.

"Hey, Lil," coach said as he pulled her to his
side,
"You don't have to get up this time, you can
retire if you'd like."

She turned and looked at the field she'd played
And at all of her teammates still in the game
She knew walking away would be far from easy,
But a choice had to be made.

the onset.

Ugly thoughts in darkened conscience
Broken pride in pretend notions
Cherry-faced and vulnerable
Officially expendable.

Safety hides frightened underneath
Surreality unveils it's sheath.
Dreams fade to colorless nightmares
Silent, dementing, full of snares.

This sickness is looming near me
Bleeding into my sanity.
It's manifesting in my brain
Scalping this lioness' mane.

Bald and bleeding, ripe and ruined
All enjoyment is now burdened.
A feeling that was natural
Now it's distant and ambrosial.

What's it called, that thing that lasts only an instance?

Happiness.

to be heard.

We stand up but look down
Avoid eyes behind fears
Ignore onslaughts of crown
Remain distant from love
and hold close to our tears
And those who look up
Stand higher than all
Demanding notice and disrupts
While promoting the wrong
How can we walk straight
If our heads are bent down
How can we live for sun
If we commit to darkness to drown
Standing to deliver is not made of pride
But hiding in the shadows
leaves opinion to die
We can't depend on the stairs
to lift us above the corrupt
Our voices are carried through air
But must rise above, loud with love,
to be heard.

ode to Easter.

The finder of the key is the roller of the stone.
The curtain split in two is the veil that was torn.
The hand who lifts the bread is the One who raised the dead.
The open tabernacle is the empty bed.
The flame that stays lit is the Living Jesus that we praise,
And the Savior we adore is the Savior that was raised.

part four.

And so she ran her final sprint and booked it to the sideline.
It wouldn't be fair to her team or to herself if she suffered by taking her time.
Coach let his team call a timeout to shout their curses and their cries
He knew that losing the quarterback would be tough for quite some time.

And yet it must be said
that the loss did not put the game on hold
Because as in life, when the timeout ends,
the game must continue on.

The second string, a bit nervous, stepped up to the game
While she had studied the plays for her whole life
She said she felt unready because without practice
The game couldn't be played right.

"Don't worry," Coach said, "I won't let you start off wrong."
He handed her Lil's old helmet and said,

"Your mother would want you to be strong."
And off she went into the game knowing she'd now always be first string.
As the clock resumed its counting down, she heard someone whispering,

"I've raised you right, I've raised you well.
I know you'll lead the team to glory.
And though I'll be here with you, watching,
Someday I can't wait to hear you tell a champion's story.

I cannot say that winning will always come easy
In fact, I know you'll make mistakes.
But what I've learned is that if you trust the Coach
He'll lead you to the end zone even if your path there isn't straight.

I love you, kid, I always have.
I've watched you start your own team and raise amazing players.
If you need me, I'll be on the bench, right here, just call me if you need me.
And while I may not always answer, as the line is often busy,
I promise to get back to you, be it through a picture or a penny."

And so in the family's football hall of fame,
There sits the the ball Lil saved,
Autographed with memories rather than a name
Right next to an empty case for trophies
For when her daughter brings home
The next victory for her family.

the end.

I came,
I tried,
I did my best.

Ink's dry,
pen's down,
I think I'll rest.

www.ingramcontent.com/pod-product-compliance
Lightning Source LLC
Chambersburg PA
CBHW051756130826
49812CB00033B/1175
9789357210508